Elizabeth Blackwell

America's First Woman Doctor

by Teri L. Tilwick

Boston, Massachusetts
Chandler, Arizona
Glenview, Illinois
Upper Saddle River, New Jersey

Illustrations
5, 6 Dan Bridy.

Photographs
Every effort has been made to secure permission and provide appropriate credit for photographic material.
The publisher deeply regrets any omission and pledges to correct errors called to its attention in subsequent editions.

Unless otherwise acknowledged, all photographs are the property of Pearson Education, Inc.

Photo locators denoted as follows: Top (T), Center (C), Bottom (B), Left (L), Right (R), Background (Bkgd)

All Photos: Library of Congress

ISBN-13: 978-0-328-67586-9
ISBN-10:   0-328-67586-5

6 7 8 9 10   V0FL 16 15 14 13

Following Her Dream

Have you ever thought about being a doctor when you grow up? Elizabeth Blackwell did. There was a problem, though. She grew up in the middle of the 1800s. Only men were doctors.

Many people back then thought women could not learn as well as men. Blackwell proved them wrong. She became the first woman doctor in the United States.

Blackwell was born in England in 1821. Her father wanted to start a business in the United States. Her family sailed to America. They settled in New York.

Blackwell's parents believed people should try to make the world a better place. One day, an older friend said Blackwell should become a doctor. She thought about it. Then she made a plan.

Blackwell applied to many **medical** schools. However, most of the schools turned her down because she was a woman.

Blackwell was turned down by medical schools because she was a woman.

Becoming a Doctor

Geneva Medical College

Geneva College in New York was different. There, teachers let the students decide. Should they let a woman come to school? The students thought it was a joke, so they all voted "yes."

Everyone was shocked when Blackwell arrived. At first, she was treated rudely by other students and by people in the town of Geneva.

Blackwell worked hard. Over time, people changed their minds. On graduation day, the audience clapped for her. She was first in her class.

Now, Blackwell needed to find a job. That was difficult. American hospitals did not want to hire a woman doctor. Blackwell went to France. In Paris she found a job in a **maternity** hospital. She enjoyed working with mothers and babies.

Doctor Elizabeth Blackwell taking care of new mothers and babies

Making a Difference

Blackwell did many things that made a difference. She adopted an **orphan** named Kitty Barry. Kitty made Blackwell's life happier. In 1857, Blackwell opened a medical center for poor women and children.

Soon after, the Civil War began. Blackwell trained nurses to help **wounded** soldiers.

Blackwell trained nurses during the Civil War.

Blackwell helped other women become doctors.

After the war ended, Blackwell opened a medical college for women. She was glad to help other women become doctors.

Blackwell spent the rest of her life in England with her daughter, Kitty. She wrote about her amazing life as America's first woman doctor. Blackwell said:

"It is not easy to be a **pioneer**, but oh, it is fascinating! I would not trade one moment, even the worst moment, for all the riches in the world."

Glossary

maternity having to do with mothers and babies

medical having to do with doctors and medicine

orphan a child without a mother or father

pioneer a person who is first to do something

wounded hurt